Mortal Coil

poems

Charles Rammelkamp

Clare Songbirds Publishing House Poetry Series
ISBN 978-1-947653-93-1
Clare Songbirds Publishing House
Mortal Coil © 2020 Charles Rammelkamp

All Rights Reserved. Permission to reprint individual poems must be obtained from the author who owns the copyright.

Printed in the United States of America
FIRST EDITION

Clare Songbirds Publishing House was established to provide a print forum for the creation of limited edition, fine art from poets and writers, both established and emerging. We strive to reignite and continue a tradition of quality, accessible literary arts to the national and international community of writers, and readers. Chapbook manuscripts are carefully chosen for their ability to propel the expansion of art and ideas in literary form. We provide an accessible way to promote the art of words in order to resonate with, and impact, readers not yet familiar with the siren song of poets and writers. Clare Songbirds Publishing House espouses a singular cultural development where poetry creates community and becomes commonplace in public places.

140 Cottage Street
Auburn, New York 13021
www.claresongbirdspub.com

Contents

Immortal	7
Eternal Youth	8
The Ambassadors	9
Gemini	10
Ch-ch-ch-Changes	11
Six Months	12
New Year's Eve, 2005	13
Yahrzeit Notices	14
Mishebarach	15
Falling Short	16
Shoelaces	17
Dress Rehearsal	18
Under the Microscope	19
Eternity	20
Tyranny Has a Witness	21
Melanoma	22
Pain Management	23
May You Be Inscribed	24
Inherit the Wind	25
You'll Be Older Too	26
Thufferin' Thuccotash	27
Getting Even	28
Fuck You, You Fucking Fuck	29
Dukkha	30
Soldier's Disease	32
Saint Vitus	33
The Body	34
Playing Doctor	35
O Muse	36
Last Wishes	37
The Cement Floor	38
Ugler Lee	39

Acknowledgements

"Gemini" – *Homestead Review*
"Dukkha," "Pain Management" – *Cicatrix Publications*
"The Cement Floor" – *Cicatrix Publications*
"Ch-ch-ch-changes," - *Plainsongs*
"A Warning Sign," - *Allegro*
"Shoelaces" – *Sheepshead Review*
"May You Be Inscribed," "Falling Short" – *Slant*
"Inherit the Wind" – *Meat for Tea*
"Yahrzeit Notices" – *Misfit Magazine*
"O Muse" – *Waterways*
"You'll Be Older Too" – *TLJ Publishing Group*
"The Ambassadors" – *Song of the San Joaquin*
"Last Wishes" – *Nerve Cowboy*
"Boo Coo" – *The 5-2 Crime Poetry*
"New Year's Eve, 2005" – *Exit 13*
"Eternity" – *South Florida Poetry Journal*
"Mishebarach" – *Iodine Poetry Journal*
"Immortal" – *Main Channel Voices*
"Ugler Lee" – *Body Verses*
"Fuck You, You Fucking Fuck" – *Broke Bohemian*
"Dress Rehearsal" – *Tipton Poetry Journal*
"Melanoma," "The Body" – *Pangolin Review*
"Saint Vitus" and "Soldier's Disease" – *Blood and Thunder*
"Thufferin' Thuccotash" and "Getting Even" (under the title, "Easy for You to Say") – *Colere*

This book is for Paloma and Emilio

Immortal

"Your Aunt Edith died young,"
Uncle Harold pointed out,
testy as a child interrupted in its nap.
"Heart attack.
And your grandfather.
He was only in his fifties, too.
Cerebral thrombosis."

Married to my father's older sister,
and already over seventy,
Uncle Harold lay in the chaise longue
in the late afternoon shade
on the porch beside the lake,
warning me, smug college student,
my life was not endless.

Looking at the liver spots
discoloring his arthritic hands,
the wrinkles in his face,
his wavy white hair,
I forgave him.

Eternal Youth

Leaving the grocery store,
I watched the old man
trying to pull himself
from the passenger seat,
left hand clutching the door,
right tight on the frame,
struggling like a beetle on its back,
his cane useless between his legs.

The car idled at the entrance,
his driver, an overweight black woman,
behind the wheel, letting him out here
before she parked the car in the lot.

"Here, you need some help?"
I put my bag of groceries down,
grabbed him by the arms, lifted
while he pushed himself to balance.

"I'm ninety-two," the man thanked me.
"I only have one friend still alive."

"I'm sixty-five," I replied,
thinking how sad his confession,
my age now a sign of vigorous youth
though I'd been feeling my mortality
all that summer, ever since
my Medicare card came in the mail
only four months before.

The Ambassadors

"That's where the hotel was,
where Bobby Kennedy was shot,"
my twin brother points
to a huge public school administration building
as we walk along Wilshire Blvd.
There's a plaque on the sidewalk honoring RFK.

"Remember that? We were in high school,
woke up on our birthday to learn
he'd been shot the night before
after winning the California primary."

"Yeah, a couple of months after Doctor King,"
I nodded, remembering our Michigan childhood.
"Then in November Nixon beat Ho-hum Humphrey
and that bigot George Wallace,
who'd also been shot that year.
Crazy times."

"The city asked the family
if it was OK to tear down the hotel," Bob says.
"The Cocoanut Grove used to be in the Ambassador, too.
All kinds of celebrities – Errol Flynn, Clark Gable,
Cary Grant, Marlene Dietrich."
He waves his hand in a big arc
to indicate the galaxy of stars.

My daughter and I are in LA
this Veterans' Day weekend
to visit my brother
who is about to start chemotherapy:
Stage Four lung cancer.
Crazy times indeed.

Gemini

You expect it and expect it and expect it,
but when death comes,
you didn't expect it at all.

Bob had been fighting cancer for years,
a losing battle against a stronger opponent,
mano-a-mano through five rounds of chemo,
radiation, opdivo, pain management,
addiction to opiates,

and all along the Cain and Abel struggle,
the Jacob and Esau conflict,
after which, one of us would still be standing,
for a little while, at least.

Seven weeks shy of sixty-four,
the Beatles' milestone for old age,
me with a grandchild on my knee,
he with a widow and pet iguana.

And a lifetime of memories,
not all good,
that I shall scrimp and save.

Ch-ch-ch-changes

Turn and face the strange.

An e-mail arrives
from my twin brother in Los Angeles,
fighting an uphill battle with cancer,
stage four. Started in his lungs;
now it's in his spine.
He's in real pain
after five bouts of chemo
over the last year and a half
and now a drug treatment called Opdivo.
No telling how much time he has left,
the last of my nuclear family,
father, mother, older brother
already dead.

An overlapping text pings my phone.
It's my daughter, on her way home
from the hospital
where she'd gone at midnight –
false labor, it turned out,
Braxton-Hicks contractions,
seismic waves ripping through the Earth –
but still less than two centimeters dilated.
Still, she's in terrific discomfort, too,
soon to deliver my first grandchild,
a girl we already call Paloma.

Six Months

When I spoke to my sister-in-law that Friday
she said the doctors had told her
six months: how much longer
her husband had to live. My twin brother.

Bob was being sent home from St. Vincent's
in Los Angeles, for hospice care.
I spoke to him briefly; he sounded exhausted.
I promised to call after he got home.

Spring Sunday in Baltimore,
the dogwoods and cherry blossoms
just coming into bloom.
Sitting on the front porch, I resolved
to call Bob later that afternoon.
I had six months, right?

But then my daughter stopped by
with her husband and baby,
out for a stroll on a lovely afternoon:
my first grandchild,
not yet three months old.

By the time they left,
it was getting to be dinner time.
I needed to tend to the lentil soup
I was preparing; I would call Bob tomorrow,
I told myself. Six months.

When I called Los Angeles the next day,
Lourdes told me he'd died early that morning.

New Year's Eve, 2005

Having come back from my first visit
to New Mexico at the start of the month,
to bury my brother David,
dead at 57 from a mysterious illness,
I've now gone through North and South
Carolina for the first time,
my wife and I driving
my mother-in-law's Toyota, recently repaired,
back up to Philly,
where she's been a refugee
at her daughter's house
since the hurricane
wiped out her retirement condo,
wrecked her car,
nearly three months before.

We're hoping to make it through
the Capital Beltway traffic
before night falls
and the drunken partiers
come out like vampires
to swoop around 495.

The year is fading
like the late-afternoon light
in the rearview mirror,
missed about as much
as the exit to Bethesda behind us.

Yahrzeit Notices

My brother's name was in the Yahrzeit list
in the synagogue's weekly Shabbat program,
two-thirds the way down the "Remembered" column,
my own in the adjacent "Relation" row:
David, brother of Charles.

I didn't recognize many of the names
in the list of the congregation's dead,
most of them identified as "father of" or "mother of";
some of the dead were grandparents
(Harold Schwartz, grandfather of Erica Levy).

But two names stood out below mine:
Joshua Rubin, son of Andy and Janet Rubin,
Amanda Rubin, daughter of Andy and Janet Rubin.
I didn't know Andy or Janet,
not to mention Joshua or Amanda,
but I could only imagine a horrible accident
in which Joshua and Amanda had been killed,
bloody and tragic, the parents' grief monumental.
Why else would a son and daughter be remembered
the very same week? Why else would parents
be remembering the deaths of their children?

My big brother David?
Dead way too young.

Mishebarach

Midway through the Torah service
the cantor offers a prayer
for those who are ill or suffering.
"May He Who has blessed our forefathers,
Avraham, Yitzchak, and Ya'akov,
bless and heal those who are ill…"
He sweeps his arms around the room
like a lighthouse searchlight swinging out
to illuminate the afflicted.
Congregants call out names.

"Harry Bergman," Rachel Goldstein murmurs
as the cantor's arm sweeps by.
"Alex Kaufman, Avi Katz, Shira Garber,"
Gilbert Stein proclaims, a rescuer
shouting after shipwrecked survivors.
"Shoshona Weiss, Sarah Mankowitz,"
Stephanie Hirsch's phlegm-choked voice croaks,
plaintive as a seagull on the beach.

I wonder at this prayer.
Do we expect miracles from the sky?
Or is it just a simple expression of concern,
a public proclamation of grief?

My cousin lies in a hospital bed in Albany,
a heart attack so massive
it's wiped out her brain function.
The cantor's hand nails me in space.
"Christie Sorum," I whisper,
feeling fraudulent, ineffectual.

His arm completes the arc;
the cantor finishes the prayer:
"May He speedily send
complete recovery from Heaven.
May their recovery be immediate and complete.
And let us say…"

"Amen," the congregation cries out,
complicit in the prayer.

Falling Short

"Rabbi, hold up!" Jimmy Schwartz calls
from the rear of the sanctuary.
Himmelfarb had just begun his Yom Kippur sermon
when one of the congregants in a rear pew
slipped to the floor,
cracking his head on a metal armrest.

In an instant, a score of people clog the aisle,
like the multitudes crossing the Red Sea,
either to help or just to see who it is.

"Get out of the aisle NOW!"
Henry Brookmeyer shouts,
his the booming voice of an archangel.
"Give him some room!"
Henry thumbs 911 on his cellphone,
barking directions into the speaker.

Milt Rudoff and Jerry Rosenthal, both physicians,
wade through the crowd
to the fallen man,
one of them already administering CPR.

I stand paralyzed against a shelf of *chumasim,*
a pillar of salt,
no less guilty in the eyes of God
than Lot's wife,
for my feckless behavior,
Jimmy and Henry and I the ushers,
only two of us acting decisively.

Shoelaces

"Oh, my shoe just came off."
Helpless, Burt sat half in,
half out of the passenger's seat
where he'd managed to wedge himself
while I stowed his walker
across the backseat.

"Here, I can get it."
I fitted the oxford back on his foot,
laced the leather strings,
looped the lace into a bow.

All the while I could feel the chagrin
oozing out of him like oil,
this frail old man
who'd once commanded rooms
full of physicians and nurses,
soothed patients with his compassion,
guiding them through
the scariest episodes of being alive.

Now defeated by shoelaces and seatbelts.

Dress Rehearsal

"Izzy was all about his D-Day exploits,"
Jacob mused. "That 'greatest generation' nonsense.
To hear him, he single-handedly saved
the world from Hitler, a real Audie Murphy."
Jacob could say this, a World War Two vet himself,
though he hadn't seen much action,
a stateside army journalist for four years,
Izzy having been in the infantry overseas.

"It was all he ever talked about,
forging his old man's signature to get in,
fighting the Germans in France."
How tiresome it was! Jacob's shrug confided.
"You knew he re-joined for Korea, right?
But apparently he was something of a goof-off.
You must've heard his story about the shenanigans
with the stolen jeep? That was Izzy,
a cocky little bastard.
Well, he dined out for seventy years
on shooting German kids as scared as he was,
you can say that much for him."

Izzy'd had a career in "the scrap metal business,"
though not even his son could say
exactly what Izzy did.
Jacob had gone on to become a doctor,
internal medicine, ran a clinic for the poor.

"Well, here we are," I said,
driving up to the funeral home entrance,
popping open the doors,
scurrying around to the passenger's side,
to position his walker, lift him out of his seat.
We were early enough, I hoped,
to get him to an aisle seat up front
where he could hear the rabbi's eulogy for Izzy,
Jacob's hearing failing along with everything else.

Under the Microscope

"The Steve Carell character complains,
'Socrates said the unexamined life
is not worth living,'" I was telling Burt
at the kiddush luncheon,
relating a joke I'd heard at the movies.
Teddy Borowitz had just rolled him up
in his wheelchair to the folding table.
"'But the examined life is no bargain either.'"

Usually morose, Burt roared, his mirth genuine,
and I understood the comedian's satisfaction,
getting an audience to laugh.

"After Miriam died, my life went to hell,"
Burt had observed more than once to me:
his wife of thirty years, killed
in a cancer treatment gone wrong.
Until then it had been all success,
the distinguished medical career,
the show-business hobby, the home,
the kids, the friendships — poets,
painters, playwrights -- the travel.

Now, helpless, he's in assisted living,
pushed around by attendants in his wheelchair,
nothing but time on his hands,
time to review his life,
to assess it and to weigh it and to size it up.

Eternity

When the young man held the elevator door for them –
he must have been in his sixties –
Etta and Blanche rolling past in their wheelchairs,
on a coquettish impulse Etta'd blurted
that he had nice legs –
he in shorts on this warm June day.

The man had blushed,
the skin on his forehead pinking
up near the gray fringe of his hair.

Now, lying in her bed, waiting for sleep,
the restraining bars up so she wouldn't roll off,
break her hip again,
she remembered a boy in her youth
admiring her legs at the beach,
how they'd flirted all afternoon by the shore,
she there with her parents on a vacation.

They'd talked and talked,
until Etta realized her skin was burnt,
the boy – was his name Tommy? –
apologizing for keeping her out in the sun
and she apologizing for having to leave his company.

Her family'd gone home the next day,
Etta's mother worried about her daughter's sunburn,
and she never saw Tommy again,
but she can hear his voice now,
lying on her back in her adult crib.
"It's all right," he'd assured her,
"We have all the time in the world."

Tyranny Has a Witness

"What's your ball cap say?"
At the Jewish nursing home
an elderly pair has just joined me
on the elevator going up.
I am here to visit a friend.

Frail as an insect,
his shirt bagging away from his thin frame
like a husk, the shrunken man,
at least a foot shorter than I, and stooped,
points up at the hat on my head
like a birdwatcher spotting a warbler.

"Tyranny has a witness," I answer.
"I got it from Human Rights Watch.
They wanted a donation."
I generally avoid bumper stickers,
t-shirts and slogan-plastered caps
for just this reason,
as if I were suddenly a spokesman
for a candidate or a cause.

The fragile old woman with him
cackles like a radio coming to life.
"It needs more than a witness,"
she declares, a once-shrill voice
gone now to a kind of static-y hum.
"It needs a bomb, or an army."

I chuckle to humor her.
My God, this elevator is slow!
That's when I see the faint numerals
tattooed on her bony wrist.

Melanoma

After the dermatologist gouged my numbed skin
for the biopsy,
scooping out the rough brown patch on my thigh
the family doctor'd seen at my check-up
a couple of weeks before –
a chocolate smudge I'd taken to be a birthmark –
told me the lab results would come back
in about a week,
I asked him what
the worst-case scenario was.

The doctor looked at a loss for words,
which I tried to interpret with a muttered,
"Death, I suppose," making a face,
doing my best to be fatalistic,
all along sure it was nothing.

"You mean you don't want to know
the best-case scenario?" he smiled.

"Well, then it's 'nothing,'" I shrugged.

"Or else it's something," he nodded.
"We'll know in a week."

Pain Management

"There's nothing quite as entertaining
as other people's pain,"
my father once observed
when the scandal of our neighbor's wife
became the main topic of town conversation,
in stores, in bars, at work,
around the dinner table.
Turned out she'd been sleeping
with her husband's boss.
Our neighbor's anguish burned, acid, electric.

I thought of this now
as my own neighbor told me
the circumstances of her "retirement"
almost a decade ago by now:
her ex-husband's second wife
her superior at the hospital.

"I could see the writing on the wall,"
Dorothy muttered, bitter as bile,
"so I signed the papers with personnel
to retire the end of June,
only another six months away.

"But Lucia wanted me out of there yesterday.
I just wanted my twenty years,
to boost my retirement check,
but she just couldn't endure me there."

All at once I saw the suffering
behind Dorothy's acerbic manner,
the crushing humiliation that must have greeted her
every morning when she opened her eyes.

"I never even bothered John" –
her voice a high whine now,
a dog that's been kicked to submission –
"just talked to his majesty the holy surgeon
if it was something about our kids.
But Lucia's hatred was a furnace blast.
In the end I had to get a lawyer."

May You Be Inscribed

"It's the first time
two men with the same last name
have hit back-to-back homeruns
in a playoff game
since Brooks and Frank Robinson,"
the sports announcer marveled
about Victor and J.D. Martinez
hitting homeruns for Detroit
in their loss last night to the Orioles.

My God, I thought,
who keeps track of these things?
True, sports is all about
breaking records, winning games,
but recording these obscure factoids,
dredging them up out of ledgers and databases?

Yom Kippur starts at sundown.
The Great Statistician in the Sky,
Who knows what each of us has done and thought
during the course of the year –
who's been naughty, who's been nice –
passes judgment on us all,
so the liturgy goes.

"On Rosh Hashanah it is written,
and on Yom Kippur it is sealed,
who will live and who will die,
who by fire, who by water...."

I've recently had a cancer removed:
my mortality on my mind.

Inherit the Wind

Our financial advisor,
a Peruvian dude named Luis,
into numbers and formulas,
not so much literary allusions,
commented about his retirement-age clients:
"A lot of these guys end up like King Lear."

What did he mean?
Money to bequeath and children all too anxious
to get their hands on it?
The kids already making plans
how to spend it all?
Naked greed turning the patriarch's heart into stone?
A lack of proper gratitude?

But Luis couldn't or wouldn't elaborate,
only suggested we shift some of our investments
to the bond market.
At our age,
no need to take too many risks.

You'll Be Older Too

What a beating teeth take.
All that chewing, biting, grinding.
No wonder they fall apart.

I remember my grandmother's dentures,
grinning skeleton in a glass by her bedside,
her cheeks sunken, mouth puckered like an asshole.

My childhood friend Alan,
his ambition to "join the service,"
have all his teeth pulled, replaced.

Now I face an implant at sixty-five,
a wobbly front tooth,
roots long dead, R.I.P.

Casualty of an accident
fifty years ago, now
hanging fanglike from my face.

Implants preserve bone,
save adjacent teeth,
cost effective, the brochure says.

On the cover a black man,
a white man, a blond woman,
dazzling dentist smiles, white coats.

Thufferin' Thuccotash

I've always been skeptical
when the dental implant commercials
come on television during news programs.
An entire mouth full of gaps and stumps
transformed into a Hollywood smile
all in one afternoon –
as if the fairy godmother
waved her wand,
changing the charwoman rags
into a sparkling ballroom gown.

"I used to run to the bathroom in tears,
having to adjust my dentures,"
the comely but not too glamorous actress declares.
"Now just look at this smile!"

"I have higher self-esteem,"
the stoic cowboy confesses.
"My new smile gives me the confidence
to find love again."

"We'll discuss financing options
during your first visit,"
the voice in the commercial confides,
making me think of car salesmen.

But when my own dead tooth is yanked –
a mercy killing –
leaving an archway entrance
into the darkness of my mouth,
to be filled with a temporary one,
the dentist tells me it will be a few months
before the bone graft,
the implant a little while later,
the crown sometime after that.

Meanwhile, though, I feel like Daffy Duck,
lisping my annoyance about growing older.

Getting Even

"Revenge is a dish best served cold,"
I joked to Marty at the gym,
and it came out sounding
like a car driving through slush,
fishtailing through the end of "revenge is,"
wet snow under the hubcaps,
shooshing through the spittle and mist
of "dish best served,"
all thanks to the temporary tooth
as plausible in my mouth
as a guest panelist on a game show.

Saul had just apologized
for taking Marty's towel
from the peg, after his shower –
an accident, gym towels identical
as my row of teeth – and Marty,
forgiving him, warned
he'd get even later.

My false tooth looks way better
than the dead one it's replaced;
but, a retainer with a tooth attached,
it causes certain unforeseen slurring.

Marty backs away from the spray,
and I resolve to be alert
to these words and phrases that highjack
my speech, as if a payback
for an innocent offense
I inadvertently committed.

Fuck You, You Fucking Fuck

I'd just removed my "flipper"
before going to bed –
the plastic retainer with the false tooth
I put into my mouth
like one of those wax Halloween candies
with the vampire fangs,
to cover the gap in my smile
where the dead tooth had been yanked –
when I saw the internet ad
for a baseball cap whose visor read:
Fuck You, You Fucking Fuck.

Snickering with adolescent mirth,
I pointed it out to my wife.
"Abby," I joked, "this is what
I want for Chanukah."
When she came over to look,
I read the slogan aloud.

Only, whistling through
the hole in my mouth,
it made me sound
like a flatulent old man,
the hiss and poof of loose bowels.

With chagrin, I recalled
my grandmother's dentures
in a glass of water
by her bedside,
her mouth collapsed to a pucker
like a deflated balloon.

That only happens to old people,
I remembered thinking at the time.

Dukkha

"Like all hairless cats,
they must be protected from the sun,"
the narrator informs us,
a TV program about felines..
Sphynx? Manx? Ukrainian Levkov?
Can't remember. Wasn't paying close attention.

A fair-skinned man,
I nevertheless always tried to get a tan,
lying on the beach in the sun,
only to get burned,
even lathered with sunscreen.
Now, decades later,
I am plagued with skin cancer,
melanoma gouged out of my leg,
basal cell carcinoma removed
from under my eye.

The dermatologist warns me to wear hats,
while also observing, "Of course,
the damage has already been done."
I look at the scars and wonder
how
much more flesh will need to be taken.
Will it add up to a pound?

But on a scale of suffering,
I recognize this is nothing.
Look at my brothers, both dead,
one from a mysterious infection at fifty-seven,
one at sixty-three after a two-year fight with cancer.

Don't we always compare ourselves
on the spectrum of suffering?
Whether from compassion or schadenfreude?
You've just had a dental implant,
but I just had a knee replacement.
My double pneumonia knocked me out
all last winter,
so don't complain to me about your allergies!

Isn't this what aging's all about,
the dents and dings along the way?
My cats lived nearly twenty years.
I remember them as kittens;
they aged visibly before my eyes.

Soldier's Disease

"Bayer's just released a safe alternative
to morphine," Doc Harrison told my mam.
The war'd been over five years,
but Grandpop still felt the pain
where his leg'd been amputated
after that Reb cannon blast
at the Battle of Spotsylvania Court House,
the year I turned ten.
Tore his leg off up to the knee,
and they had to saw it off in mid-thigh,
fitted him with a peg leg.

Daddy'd already been killed at Fredericksburg
two years before.
All he'd left us?
About three hundred in real estate
and a couple of horses.
Mam had to ask the Pension Bureau
to pay funeral costs.

"Name comes from the German for 'heroic,'"
Doc went on, "heroisch."
He filled the hypodermic,
cleansed a patch of skin on Grandpop's arm
with a piece of cotton and some alcohol.
"This new drug heroin'll be a lot safer
than the morphine he's been injecting.
Won't have that craving's been driving him wild
these past six or seven years,
and no need to worry about losing his service pension,"
Doc added, looking at us like Santa Claus.

Saint Vitus

When my genealogist friend told me
she'd traced my family back to Aachen, Germany,
fourteenth century, as if following my lifeline
from my palm all the way to my heart,
I thought maybe I now understood
where my Sydenham's chorea came from –
"a neurological manifestation of rheumatic fever,"
the doctors lectured, blanketing my "involuntary movements"
in a wool of words: "an autoimmune process
triggered by the presence of beta-hemolytic streptococci."

It all started at the annual "Saint V Dance"
at Potawatomi Rapids High, the end of June
my junior year. The DJ spun a 45,
Mitch Ryder and the Detroit Wheels singing
"Little Latin Lupe Lu."
I was doing the Watusi with Marybeth Montag,
but I couldn't stop when the song ended.
Marybeth fled in embarrassment as I continued to jerk my arms,
running away like a cat spooked by sudden movement.

My mother scolded me for my "stunt,"
dancing nonstop all night
until I fell from exhaustion,
had to be carried home on a stretcher.

But when it happened again a few years later in college,
and every so often after that
until I broke my hip one night,
I consulted the family physician,
and then it was an escalation up the ladder
of medical experts. First came the antibiotics,
the cardiac testing, the cerebrospinal fluid analysis,
the neuroimaging, the neurologists muttering
sage cryptic phrases about "evolving interventions."

Now in my sixties, I want to believe
it's the curse of that Sicilian saint
first witnessed in medieval Germany
before spreading across Europe, England, to Madagascar.
Sounds so much more romantic, and besides,
now I feel much closer to my roots.

The Body

Muriel's upset stomach turned out to be
a twenty-two-pound tumor in her intestine.
How your body seduces and betrays you,
strings you along with pleasure and sensation,
only to deceive you, leave you in pain.

Keep brushing and flossing your teeth.
They'll rot and fall out one day regardless.

Wouldn't it be better, after all,
to lose your mind first,
so you wouldn't be aware
you were falling apart?

Muriel's best friend in the nursing home,
Soledad, is sinking in the quicksand of Alzheimer's.
Can't remember a thing.
Muriel tells her over and over again
who Frosty is –
Soledad's son who visits twice a month.

Playing Doctor

Third-year medical student on rotations,
I'm working in the university hospital,
pretending to be a doctor.
That's what it feels like, anyway.
The hardest part? Actually listening.

I'm following a patient with metastatic cancer,
a man in his sixties who came in
with huge masses on his neck –
enlarged lymph nodes.
The doctors want to know where the cancer started
before it spread to the lymph nodes,
to get some kind of clue about the prognosis.
I just watch and learn.

The patient doesn't know yet he has cancer.
We don't want to tell him
until we know something more about it.
I'm only an observer now
but I feel like I have a huge secret,
an anchor in my heart, dreading
having to break the bad news.

I remember last week meeting
with a different patient and his family.
Everybody wailed when we broke the news:
incurable cancer, only weeks to live.

"Oh, God," the future widow moaned,
her face crumpling like the wad of tissue
she squeezed in her fist.
"What can we do? What are we going to do?"

Took me a minute to realize what she'd said,
the oncologist already offering comfort.
I felt like I'd dropped the ball,
not that anybody noticed.

O Muse

"At least you should get
a couple of good poems out of this,"
Mary Alice consoled
when I told her about
my cousin's suicide.

She didn't mean it
in a grave-robbing sort of way;
more like a tribute
to the enormity of the event,
as if the poet's burden
to mine experience for nuggets
of poignant detail
were a sort of monument-building.

But still, it struck me
as the last thing that mattered.
When I thought of Teddy
shooting himself in the town cemetery
a thousand miles west of me,
my mother calling with the news,
eight hundred miles to the north,
my brother on the opposite coast
acknowledging the tragedy,
cousins overseas writing to share
their shock, astonishment, distress –
the world shrank to the size of a pea,
and all we did in it –
the working, the fighting,
the fucking, the crying –
so microscopic as to be invisible.

Last Wishes

"No!" Miriam declared, shaking her head,
emphatic as a judge laying down the law.
"I don't care what Milton asked for,
it's simply not dignified."

"But Ma! Dad worshipped the guy!
You know that. You remember
how he wept like a baby
the day Johnny Unitas died.
I'd never seen him cry before."

"Your father was a respected doctor, Barry.
His patients adored him.
Colleagues from around the world
consulted him, sought his opinion.
I simply will not allow him to be buried
wearing some football player's uniform."

"Oh, Ma! It's just the jersey!
Old number nineteen with the shoulder stripes.
It's not like we're having an open casket viewing.
Nobody will ever know."

"I'll know, Barry,
and I'm putting my foot down here.
My Milton will not be buried
looking like a child worshipping a sports idol!
Besides, I'm sure there must be something
in the Torah forbidding it.

"And would it have killed him
to ask for the tie I gave him
on our wedding anniversary?"
she muttered as an afterthought.

The Cement Floor

"Death waits for these things as a cement floor waits for a dropping lightbulb." – Saul Bellow, *Herzog*

Marla arranged the home hospice care,
the palliative services,
nurses, aides, the lawyer, the insurance,
and, yes, the priest,
his soft insect body sheathed in wings.
She knew her mother believed.

Marla's mom had always berated her,
sarcastic, abusive, sneering
at Marla's three husbands,
one after the other; her childless bed,
the hippie lifestyle,
veiled references to drugs, free love.
How Marla had hated her then.

Now she was meeting with the social workers,
nurses, aides, the caseworker, the dietician,
there to find ways to feed her mother
despite the intestinal blockage –
cancer all over the place.

Marla fielded the calls, sympathy
from old friends, distant relatives,
this business of grief so exhausting.

Sometimes she wished her mother dead,
a swift end, but was it to spare her mother
or to spare herself?
Marla knew how much
she was going to miss her.

It all seemed so endless.
the way you sometimes feel in a dream,
and winter on the way now,
already October, leaves falling.

Ugler Lee

"Ugler lee," my father groaned,
frown lines breaking out around his mouth,
scratching his head, private commentary
when something unspeakable happened –
cataclysmic weather events, irreversible illness,
tragic, pointless death –
a kind of onomatopoeic observation
for something for which there are no words.

The night my grandmother died, Christmas Eve 1970,
we'd all sat down to a somber feast
on what was meant to be a festive occasion,
but nobody had much of an appetite,
waiting, waiting for a sign,
as if magi seeking a guiding star.
After dinner, my mother discovered
her mother was no longer breathing
upstairs in the room in which she lay.

"Ugler lee," my father muttered,
forehead going to wrinkles
as if a window pane struck by a rock,
picking up the phone to dial the doctor.

Charles Rammelkamp is Prose Editor for BrickHouse Books in Baltimore, where he lives, and he is the Reviews Editor for *The Adirondack Review*. For ten years he edited *The Potomac*, an online literary journal – http://thepotomacjournal.com. His photographs, poetry, fiction and reviews have appeared in many literary journals. His latest books include a collection of poems called *Mata Hari: Eye of the Day* (Apprentice House, Loyola University), and another poetry collection, *American Zeitgeist*, poems about the life and times of William Jennings Bryan, also published by Apprentice House, as well as several poetry chapbooks – *Jack Tar's Lady Parts* (Main Street rag Publishing) and *Me and Sal Paradise* (FutureCycle Press). He is the author of a novel (*The Secretkeepers*, Red Hen Press), two collections of short fiction (*A Better Tomorrow*, PublishAmerica, *Castleman in the Academy*, March Street Press), two other full-length collections of poetry (*The Book of Life*, March Street Press, *Fusen Bakudan*, Time Being Books). Two full-length collections are forthcoming from Apprentice House – *Catastroika* and from Kelsay Books – *Ugler Lee*. The cover art is by Abby Rammelkamp and is called *Faces Come out of the Rain*.

www.ingramcontent.com/pod-product-compliance
Lightning Source LLC
Chambersburg PA
CBHW062040120526
44592CB00035B/1803